KNOW
THE FACTS

DIET

Judith Anderson

WAYLAND

First published in 2008
by Wayland

Copyright © Wayland 2008

Wayland
338 Euston Road
London NW1 3BH

Wayland Australia
Level 17/207 Kent Street
Sydney, NSW 2000

Series editor: Nicola Edwards
Consultant: David Ferguson
Designer: Rawshock Design
Picture researcher: Kathy Lockley
Artwork by Ian Thompson

Pictures of young people posed by models. The author and publisher would like to
thank the models and the following for allowing their pictures to be reproduced in
this publication: Gyori Antoine/Corbis Sygma: 25; BSIP, Laurent/Science Photo
Library: 32; Collect/PA Archive/PA Photos: 37; Andy Crawford/Wayland Archive: 8,
26, 27, 45T; Martin Jepp/zefa/Corbis: 43; MM Productions/Corbis: 33; Ulrike
Preuss/Photofusion Photo Library: 7; Reuters/Corbis: 42; Klaus Rose/Das
Photoarchiv/Still Pictures: 41; Dieter Telemans/Panos Pictures: 9; Wishlist:
COVER, 4, 5, 10, 11, 13-23, 28-31, 34, 36-38, 45B

British Library Cataloguing in Publication Data

Anderson, Judith (Judith Mary)
   Diet. - (Know the facts)
   1. Diet - Juvenile literature
   2. Nutrition - Juvenile
   literature
   I. Title
   613.2

ISBN: 978 0 7502 5385 7

Printed in China

Wayland is a division of Hachette Children's Books,
an Hachette Livre UK company
www.hachettelivre.co.uk

CONTENTS

FOOD FOR LIFE

We all need food. We need it for energy, for growth, and also because food is a source of pleasure and well-being. Food gives us life!

Eating a meal with family and friends is a great way to refuel and relax at the same time.

Feeling hungry

When did you last feel hungry? How could you tell? Food gives us the energy we need to grow, move, keep warm, and keep organs such as our hearts, lungs and brains working properly. If we don't eat for a few hours, we begin to feel hunger pangs in our stomachs and we may feel tired, or irritable, or less able to concentrate.

HAVE YOUR SAY

"Chips aren't healthy, but I love them!"

"I always feel hungry during maths."

"I hate tomatoes, but I like tomato sauce."

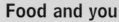

What we eat

Of course, not all food is good for us. We may eat more than we need, and sometimes we may eat the 'wrong' types of food. In fact, what we eat can seriously affect our long-term health. Choosing a varied, well-balanced diet is one way to help protect against heart disease, cancer, diabetes and a whole range of physical and psychological problems. You will be asked to think about your own eating habits at various stages throughout this book.

Food and you

What do you like to eat? Is it 'healthy'? Perhaps you prefer snacks and 'junk' food? Most people have likes and dislikes, favourite foods and things they hate. There are many reasons for this. Lifestyle, culture, the availability of certain foods and advertising all play a part. Understanding these influences can help you to make more informed choices about food.

What Would you do? ?

You are on your way home for dinner when your friend offers you a chocolate bar. Do you:

a) eat it;
b) refuse it;
c) save it for after dinner?

Turn to page 47 for the answers.

Fancy that chocolate bar? Most of us like a sugary snack sometimes. But what influences our choice? Is it hunger, convenience or habit, or the manufacturer's advertising?

WHAT HAPPENS WHEN WE EAT?

The food we eat provides us with the nutrients and the energy we need to live. So how does the food on your plate find its way into each of the billions of cells in your body?

Digestion

Digestion is the process by which food is broken down into tiny particles, or molecules. It starts as soon as food enters the mouth, as it is chewed by teeth and mixed with saliva and special acid (enzymes) in the stomach. The partly digested food is then pushed into the gut (intestines), where it is broken down even further.

Absorption

Absorption is the process by which the tiny food molecules pass through the intestinal wall and into the bloodstream. These molecules are then carried around the body in the blood, and delivered to wherever they are needed.

Waste

Our bodies cannot use every bit of the food we eat. Things like wholegrain husks, vegetable fibre and seeds are too hard to break down, so they move along to the end of the intestines and pass out of the body when we go to the toilet. This isn't really 'waste' food though — the stuff we can't digest helps keep our guts healthy and active.

Digestion begins when food enters the mouth. It is chewed and mixed with saliva.

Chewed food is swallowed and passes down the oesophagus.

It is broken down by enzymes in the stomach.

Further digestion takes place in the intestines.

The food molecules are now small enough to pass through the wall of the intestines and into the bloodstream.

Any undigested food passes out of the body.

'Is it better to eat three full meals a day or five or six smaller meals and snacks?

The best time to eat is when you feel hungry, but before you feel ravenous! The number of times you eat may depend on your particular circumstances (your age, how active you are and family habits) but the danger of too many snacks and smaller meals is that you choose quick, 'junk' foods and eat them on the go, rather than taking the time to consider whether your diet is balanced and healthy. Also, remember your teeth! The more frequently you eat or drink anything other than water, the more your teeth are exposed to damaging acid and bacteria.

If you want to avoid indigestion, sit down at mealtimes and eat slowly. It is also a good idea to avoid fizzy drinks as they are full of gas that can give you indigestion, and sweeteners that are bad for your teeth. They may also reduce your appetite for the nutritious food on your plate.

Help yourself

Eating tips!

• Do you ever get an uncomfortable feeling in your stomach when you have eaten too much, or too quickly? This is indigestion, and is best avoided by sitting down, eating slowly and chewing carefully.

• Eating slowly also gives your brain time to recognise that your stomach is filling up. If you eat too quickly, you may eat more than you need.

• Try not to skip meals. Eating at regular times stops you becoming so hungry that you then overeat!

FOOD GROUPS

When the food we eat enters the intestines it breaks down into different types of food molecules, or nutrients. The main types of nutrients are proteins, carbohydrates, fats, vitamins and minerals. (There is fibre and water too; these are examined on pages 10-11.) Each nutrient has a specific job to do inside the body.

Proteins

Proteins are the body's building blocks – vital for growth and repair. They are found in meat, fish, dairy products, nuts and pulses such as beans and lentils.

Eggs are a good source of protein, as well as some vitamins and minerals.

Carbohydrates

Carbohydrates provide energy. They come in two types: simple, and complex. Simple carbohydrates are found in naturally sweet foods such as fruit and table sugar. They are absorbed very quickly into the bloodstream, providing a quick 'hit' of energy that doesn't last long. Complex carbohydrates are digested more slowly, and therefore release energy over a longer period of time. They are found in wholegrain bread, pasta, potatoes and rice.

WHAT'S THE PROBLEM?

"My mum has diabetes. What is it?"

Diabetes occurs when the body cannot process sugar properly. In a healthy person, sugar is processed with the help of a substance called insulin. In a diabetic person, the body has stopped producing insulin which means that sugar builds up in the blood, causing health problems. While there is no 'cure' for diabetes, the symptoms can be treated with insulin injections and a carefully controlled diet.

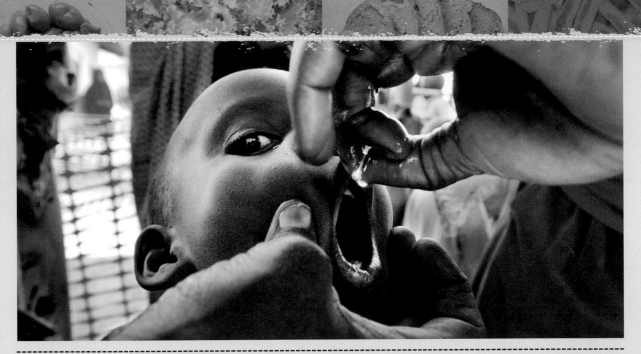

This child is being given vitamin A drops. A lack of vitamin A is a common cause of sight problems amongst children with very poor diets.

Fat

Fat also provides energy and helps other nutrients do their jobs. However, eating too much fat means it builds up in the body and causes health problems. Saturated fats (found in meat and dairy produce) and hydrogenated fats (oil that has been processed) are particularly bad for us because they increase cholesterol which causes heart disease.

Vitamins and minerals

There are many different vitamins and minerals and each has a particular job to do. They are found in a wide variety of foods such as vegetables, dairy products, meat, fish and whole grain products. However, some vitamins cannot be stored in the body, so in order to stay healthy we have to eat foods containing them every day.

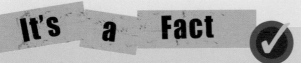 It's a Fact ✓

Salt (a mineral) is an essential part of our diet. However, too much salt raises the blood pressure, which can lead to heart problems. Experts say we should eat no more than one small teaspoon of salt a day, but many food companies add a lot of salt to foods such as bread, cereals, cheese and processed food such as baked beans, because salt has a strong flavour and increases sales. A single pizza may contain over twice as much salt as the entire recommended daily amount for a 10-year-old child.

WATER AND FIBRE

A healthy body needs a healthy transport system so that nutrients can move around the body in the most efficient way. There are two essential ingredients for this: water and fibre.

 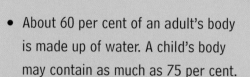
Water

Water helps food move through the gut and is the main substance in blood. In fact, water is an essential part of every single cell in the body; without it, we would die. Yet our bodies are losing water all the time, when we go to the toilet, when we sweat, even when we breathe. So it is vital that we top up our water levels regularly.

Experts say that we should drink at least eight glasses of water each day. However, while all drinks contain water, they may also contain sugar, caffeine, or artificial sweeteners or flavours. Pure water is best. And it is free!

Help yourself

Drink water!

Studies show that regularly drinking water at school helps children concentrate more and perform better.

- Make sure that you keep a water bottle with you at all times.
- Don't wait until you feel thirsty – this means you are already dehydrated (lacking in water).
- Remember that if the weather is hot, or you are exercising, then you need more than eight glasses of water a day in order to replace what you lose through sweat.
- Don't waste your money on expensive bottled water – fill up from the tap!

Fruit and vegetables are full of fibre.

Fibre

Fibre is found in all fruit, vegetables, seeds and wholegrains such as rice and wheat. It is not a nutrient and is not absorbed into the bloodstream, but it is essential for a healthy digestive system. Its job is to keep food moving along the intestines and also to stop any unhealthy bacteria from building up in the gut. A diet low in fibre can cause constipation and more serious types of bowel disease.

Adding more fibre to your diet is easy. Choose foods high in whole grains such as wholemeal bread and try to eat at least five portions of fruit and vegetables each day. Don't peel them if you can help it. Eating an apple or a carrot or a potato without peeling off the skin can increase its fibre content by as much as 50 per cent. Just make sure you wash them first.

HAVE YOUR SAY

"Baked beans are full of fibre!"

"I love a stir-fry with lots of crunchy vegetables!"

A BALANCED DIET

Vitamins, protein, carbohydrate, fibre – how do you know if you are eating enough of the things your body needs? And how do you make sure you don't eat too much?

Guideline daily amount (GDA)

The guideline daily amount, or GDA is the amount that experts agree is the right quantity of any particular food group to meet your daily needs. Sometimes this actually appears as weight in grams on food labels (see pages 16-17), but in fact there is an easy way to obtain a rough idea.

Imagine that all the food you eat in a single day is sitting on a plate. A balanced diet would divide up into one-third fruit and vegetables, one-third complex carbohydrates (bread, pasta, potatoes),

just under one-sixth dairy (milk, cheese and yoghurt), just under one-sixth meat, fish, eggs or vegetarian alternatives, and a small fraction for sweet and fatty foods.

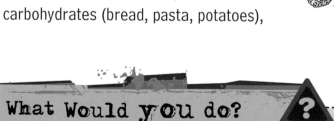

What Would you do? ?

You wake up late on a school day. Do you:

a) buy a snack bar from the vending machine at school;
b) miss the bus while your mum cooks you a fried breakfast;
c) eat a bowl of whole grain cereal, drink a glass of water and grab an apple to eat on the way?

Turn to page 47 for the answers.

Is there a vending machine in your school or youth club? What kinds of drinks and snacks are in it? Where would they sit on the food plate on page 12?

Variety

Another way to get all the nutrients you need is to aim for as much variety throughout the day as possible. For example, if you eat a lot of processed food, you may not be getting enough vitamins and minerals and you're probably eating too much salt and sugar. If you eat a lot of fried food, you're almost certainly eating too much fat. On the other hand, if all you eat is apples and tomatoes

you won't be getting enough protein or the vitamin B2 which is mainly found in milk, fish and leafy green vegetables.

If you eat a wide range of fresh foods, avoid too much sugar, salt and fat and drink plenty of water you'll feel great.

WHAT'S THE PROBLEM?

'My mum says healthy food is too expensive and she doesn't have time to cook fresh food from scratch.'

'Healthy' food is an industry, just like processed food. If you buy avocados that have been imported from Kenya in expensive packaging then they will cost more than processed food such as a tin of spaghetti hoops.

However, healthy food doesn't have to be expensive, and it doesn't have to take long to prepare. How about a tomato omelette with a green salad on the side? Or a baked potato topped with tuna and sweetcorn? Both are quick and cheap to make with a good balance of food groups, plenty of fibre and not too much fat, sugar or salt. They're tasty, too.

CALORIES

A calorie is a unit of energy. Our bodies use energy all the time, even when we are asleep. But the more active we are, the more energy we use and the more calories we need. We get these calories from food.

Burning calories

Protein, carbohydrate and fat all contain calories. When we eat these foods the energy is released into our bodies and either used ('burnt'), or stored. We all burn energy continuously as our muscles contract, our heart pumps blood, our lungs move in and out and so on. We burn even more calories when we exercise, so the more we run, swim or play football, the more calories we burn. However, if we eat more calories than we burn, the extra is stored in the body as fat.

Vigorous skipping is one of the fastest ways to burn calories.

- The average chocolate covered biscuit contains around 130 calories. So does one banana, or one small slice of pizza or 10 tomatoes.

- How can you burn 130 calories? You could walk for 45 minutes, or cycle for 30 minutes. Alternatively, you could go to sleep for two hours!

Calorie counting

Too much fat in the body is not healthy. It causes health problems such as heart disease, high blood pressure and diabetes. So it is important to eat only as many calories as your body needs. People need different amounts, depending on their height, age, whether they are male or female and how physically active they are. However, most children aged between 10 and 13 need 1600 - 2000 calories each day.

Food labels often show the number of calories contained in a serving (shown as kcal or kilocalories) but another way of calculating this is to remember that there are four calories in every gram of protein or carbohydrate, and nine calories in every gram of fat.

Try calculating the number of calories you eat in any single day.

A can of cola contains around the same number of calories as a fruit smoothie. But a smoothie also contains fibre, vitamins and minerals.

WHAT'S THE PROBLEM?

'Are low calorie drinks better for you?'

A regular cola or fruit drink may contain around 150 calories. Low calorie drinks are made with artificial sweeteners instead of sugar, and are therefore much less fattening because they contain fewer calories. The absence of sugar also means they contribute less to tooth decay. However, most 'low cal' drinks (and snacks) contain very little that is actually good for you. Instead they usually contain artificial sweeteners, flavourings or other additives that you really don't need. Stick to water and you can't go wrong!

READ THE LABEL

Some food packaging bombards us with information. Lists of ingredients and a nutritional breakdown in the form of tables, or wheels, provide us with lots of detail but they aren't always easy to understand. And sometimes the messages can be misleading.

Check the label on food packaging to see if there are any 'hidden' ingredients such as salt and sugar.

Nutrition information

Most food packaging now gives a breakdown of the calories, fat, sugar, carbohydrate, salt and protein in a particular food item. It may be shown as a 'per 100g' number, or a 'per serving' number. It may also show the guideline daily amount (GDA). Such packaging can still be confusing though. For example, the labelling on cake packaging may state that the cake inside contains 'lots' of energy, and not much fat. Sounds good? Not when you look at the list of ingredients. The main ingredient is likely to be glucose/fructose syrup (a sugar). This means that the cake is high in sugar, and too much sugar will be stored in the body as fat.

Different types of fat

Remember that all fat and oil is high in calories, but some fats and oils are particularly unhealthy because they are high in cholesterol, which is bad for the heart. Cholesterol-raising products are those containing trans-fats, or saturated fat, or hydrogenated fat. Fatty meat is also high in cholesterol.

What does it mean?

You want a snack and see two different packs of crisps. The first packet says '70% less fat!' on the front. You check the label and it says '99 calories per serving'. The second packet says 'no artificial flavours or colours' and 'made with sunflower oil - low in saturated fat' - but it also says '190 calories per serving' because the fat content is still very high. However a careful look shows that the first packet contains much more salt per 100g than the second packet. Also, a 'serving' of the first packet is only 25g but a 'serving' of the second packet is 40g. So, these are your choices:

- a 25g serving of crisps high in salt but lower in fat;
- a 40g serving of crisps high in fat but lower in salt per gram and made with natural ingredients;
- a low fat, low salt snack such as an apple with no complicated label to read!

Food labels vary in the amount of infomation they give and in the way they present this information. What sorts of information would you like to see on food labels?

Too much salt is bad for us. Yet food labels don't always list salt; sometimes they list sodium instead. And they don't explain that you have to multiply the amount of sodium by two and a half to get the salt figure. Remember that food manufacturers want you to buy their product. So they may try to show that a food item is better for you than is actually the case.

HAVE YOUR SAY

"Fruit has sugar in it. Why don't they label that?"

"I don't look at labels. I don't want to know what's in my food."

PROCESSED FOOD

Processed food is the opposite of fresh food. It is food that has been pre-prepared, cooked, and then sealed, tinned or frozen in order to make it easier to transport, store and use at home. It often contains unfamiliar ingredients such as sodium benzoate, corn syrup or E111. But what are all these 'additives' and why are they in your ice cream?

Additives

An additive is a substance added to food to make it last longer (preservative), or taste nicer (flavouring or artificial sweetener), or bind together better (gelling or raising agent), or look more attractive (colouring). Sometimes vitamins and minerals are added too.

Additives can play an important part in food production, preventing food from going off and making it cheaper to produce. Artificial sweeteners in particular can help diabetics and overweight people avoid dangerous amounts of natural sugar. However, some additives, particularly E-numbers, have been linked to health problems, such as hyperactivity in children.

Frozen 'ready meals' can be stored for longer but may contain lots of additives.

Fresh or processed?

Many people choose processed food over fresh food because it is quick to prepare, it can be stored in fridges and cupboards for

WHAT'S THE PROBLEM?

'Eating fresh food means shopping more often, doesn't it?'

Not necessarily. If you plan ahead you can prepare more food than you need and freeze it yourself. Homemade pizzas, casseroles, pasta sauces and curries are all perfect for this kind of preparation, providing you with 'ready meals' without the extra sugar, salt and fat that goes into the supermarket varieties.

longer and sometimes it is cheaper. They also become used to its artificially strong flavours. However, processed food often contains surprisingly high levels of sugar, salt and fat, as well as lower levels of vitamins and fibre.

Flavouring

Did you know that many 'savoury' processed foods actually contain sugar? Take a look at the list of ingredients on a ready meal or a tin of beans or spaghetti. Sugar will be there in some form – though it might not be obvious at first. Dextrose, fructose and corn syrup are all forms of sugar. It is added to make the product more appealing to people who are used to highly flavoured foods. Salt, or a savoury substance known as monosodium glutamate, is added for the same reason.

What Would you do?

Your favourite frozen pizza is full of fat, salt and sugar, with little protein, vitamins or fibre. Do you:

a) make your own with a wholegrain base, fresh toppings and a salad on the side;

b) choose a different brand that is lower in fat;

c) have it with chips?

Turn to page 47 for the answers.

Cooking food yourself means that you know exactly what goes into it.

WHERE DOES FOOD COME FROM?

The food debate isn't just about what goes into food. Other factors may influence what we choose to eat. Where has it come from? How has it been produced? Has it travelled far? And does any of this actually make a difference?

Food crops grown locally have less distance to travel to the shops where they're sold.

Organic food

Organic food is food which has been grown or produced without the use of chemicals, including pesticides and antibiotics. Organic food is becoming more and more popular as people worry about the health risks from chemicals and the damage they cause to the environment. However, it does mean that farmers have to find other ways of protecting their crops and animals from disease, and this can add to the cost.

It's a Fact

GM crops are grown from seeds that have been 'genetically modified' to improve them in some way, often by making them more resistant to disease. In the USA, over 60 per cent of all maize is now GM. However, Europeans tend to worry more about the long-term impact of such genetic engineering and only about 2 per cent of maize grown in Europe is from GM seed.

Fair trade

Poorer farmers in developing countries are often pressured into selling their produce to big international companies at very low prices. 'Fair trade' means that a big company promises to pay farmers a fair, 'living' wage for their produce. It may mean that items such as coffee, tea, rice and chocolate that carry the Fairtrade mark are a little more expensive, but the extra money can make a huge difference to the farmers who produce them.

Local or long-haul?

We all like to buy the food we want, when we want it, but this comes at a cost to the environment. Bananas, for example, need a warm climate, and if people in the UK want to eat them then they have to be imported from somewhere like the Caribbean. Some people think that we should only eat locally produced food to cut down on greenhouse gases produced by long-haul food miles. Others argue that this would put poorer

These fresh food have been transported from Africa and South America to shops in the UK. How far has the food that you've eaten today travelled?

farmers in developing countries out of business. Try looking at the 'country of origin' labels on the food in your fridge. How far has it travelled? Is it worth it?

HAVE YOUR SAY

"The organic vegetables we get always have mud on them!"

"Fair trade chocolate is a bit more expensive but it makes it more of a treat."

I'M NOT EATING THAT!

So, you know what's good for you and what's not. Yet knowing that a particular food is healthy doesn't necessarily mean that you like to eat it. Some people say they hate the taste of avocados. Or the smell of fish. Or the texture of cheese. But have you ever wondered why they hate it?

Childhood habits

Many of our ideas about food are formed when we are very young. Some experts think that the foods our mothers ate before we were born influence our food preferences. Certainly, familiarity plays a part. The more we taste a particular flavour, the more we get used to it, and accept it. Do you enjoy trying lots of foods, or do you avoid new tastes and textures? Try making a list of any foods you don't like. Can you say why you don't like them?

What Would you do?

You hate fish, but tonight it is the only thing on the menu.
Do you:

a) refuse to eat it;
b) try a little bit;
c) disguise it with a big dollop of ketchup?

Turn to page 47 for the answers.

Vegetables come in all shapes, textures and flavours. What's your favourite?

Help yourself

Play the taste game

Choose a food you don't like but wish you did. Tomatoes, for example. Do you peel them off your pizza? Do you pick them out of sandwiches? The taste game is about re-training your tastebuds and re-thinking your ideas.

First, go out and buy some tomatoes. Choose the ones that look most appealing. Then carry out a survey amongst your friends. How do they like to eat them? Raw and whole? Sliced in a salad? Grilled with garlic and a drop of olive oil? Pureed in a pasta sauce? Find a recipe that uses them with other foods you do like. Then prepare them yourself. If you (with a friend) eat a little bit each day for one week, you will probably find that they start to taste okay – and maybe even pretty good!

Picky eaters

Experts estimate that about one-fifth of us eat no more than 10 different foods. There are two problems with this. First, it is much more difficult to eat a nutritionally well balanced diet, with a full range of vitamins and minerals, if we have only 10 foods to choose from. Second, it gets very boring! Variety makes food so much more interesting. It makes it easier to eat out with friends, share food with others, and have fun in the kitchen.

FOOD AND TRADITION

Tradition plays a huge part in the range of foods we eat. This may be a result of religion, culture or simple geography. Muslims don't eat pork, Japanese people enjoy the strong tastes of soy and wasabi, and Europeans tend to eat a lot of dairy products. Yet most cultures and traditions use foods that are both nutritionally varied and well worth trying out.

Local variations

The varied nature of food around the world is due in large part to variations in geography and climate. For example, bread and pasta is a staple source of carbohydrate in Europe and America, because wheat grows well in a temperate climate. Spicy foods are common in hot countries where chilli, pepper and cumin thrive. Countries with a sea coast tend to consume more fish, and flash-cooked or stir-fried dishes originated in China where wood for fires was scarce.

Religious traditions

Some religions deliberately avoid certain types of food. For example, Orthodox Jewish people choose not to eat pork or bacon. They also follow 'kosher' practices, which means that meat and dairy products are produced in a particular way and prepared and eaten separately. Muslims don't eat pork or bacon either, and their methods of meat production are known as 'halal'. Some Christians do not eat meat of any kind on traditional 'fasting' days.

HAVE YOUR SAY

"We always eat turkey at Christmas."

"I'm a Hindu and I don't eat beef or pork."

"My granny always eats fish on Fridays."

"I'm not Jewish, but I love chicken soup with matzo balls!"

A Jewish family gathers to celebrate a Shabbat, or Sabbath, meal during Passover.

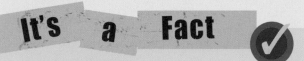

It's a Fact ✔

Ramadan is a period of inner reflection and fasting undertaken by Muslims for one month each year. It isn't a total ban on food and drink, but adult Muslims do refrain from eating or drinking anything during daylight hours. So all food must be eaten before dawn or after dusk each day. However, children, the elderly and the sick are not expected to fast as they need a more frequent intake of calories.

VEGETARIANISM

A vegetarian is someone who does not eat meat. This includes red meat, poultry such as chicken, and fish. However, most vegetarians do eat eggs and milk products such as cheese and yoghurt.

Becoming a vegetarian

There are many different reasons why people choose not to eat meat. For some, their religion forbids it or discourages it. Others are concerned about the welfare of animals reared for the table. Many think that a vegetarian diet is a healthier option because it cuts out a lot of saturated fat. Environmentalists often argue that it is better for the planet because cattle and pigs require a huge amount of land that could be kept as forest or used for crops. And some people simply don't like meat.

These kebabs are made with tofu instead of meat. Tofu is made from soya beans and is a good source of protein.

A healthy choice?

Vegetarians must make sure their daily diet is nutritionally well balanced in exactly the same way as someone who eats meat. Because meat is a good source of protein and some minerals such as calcium and iron, vegetarians need to make sure that

WHAT'S THE PROBLEM?

'I want to become a vegetarian but my dad says I won't get enough protein.'

Whether or not you eat meat should be your choice. However, your dad needs to be reassured that you will still get all the nutrients you need. Have you tried talking things through with him? If the rest of the family eats meat it may take a bit of organising to ensure that there are plenty of well-balanced alternatives for you. A variety of dairy products, eggs, beans, nuts, and pulses such as lentils should take care of the protein, but it might make things easier if you help your dad shop for them, or find some easy recipes to convince him that you aren't going to starve!

they are getting enough of these food groups from other sources. Nuts, beans and lentils, cheese and eggs are all good sources of protein, while leafy green vegetables such as cabbage and broccoli and most dairy products are good sources of calcium and iron.

Vegans

A vegan is someone who doesn't eat any animal products, including all dairy products. They also avoid foods that contain gelatine as this is made from animal bones. A vegan diet can be very healthy if it contains sufficient protein from nuts, wholegrains, pulses and beans but vegans do have to be particularly careful to ensure they get enough of all the different minerals usually found in animal products.

Couscous (a type of pasta) with butterbeans, tomatoes and peppers provides carbohydrate, protein, and a variety of vitamins and minerals.

It's a Fact

Peas, beans and lentils are a group of edible plant seeds known as pulses. There are lots of different kinds, but all are high in protein, carbohydrate and fibre and low in fat.

What Would you do?

Which of the following meals would you choose as the most nutritionally balanced for a young vegetarian?

a) baked potato with cheese;
b) three-bean salad with grated carrot and wholemeal bread and butter;
c) chips and tinned baked beans.

Turn to page 47 for the answers.

THE EATING HABIT

Do you always eat popcorn at the cinema? For many of us, eating is not just about providing ourselves with nutrients. We have learned from a young age to associate it with specific times of day, or moods, or activities. Food becomes a habit, whether we are hungry or not.

Snacking

Snacks are part of the way we live our lives. It isn't always possible to sit down to three square meals a day. Breakfast may be a quick slice of toast as we rush out the door. This means we feel hungry by mid-morning, and a snack helps us keep going until lunch. Some snacks are fine – a few nuts, a banana or a small piece of cheese give us energy and some extra protein, vitamins and minerals. But many ready-made snacks provide nothing more nutritious than a burst of sugar or a salty fix. They aren't filling and they just make us want more.

Snacking while studying can be a hard habit to break. If you replace crisps and biscuits with fruit and nuts, you might find they make you feel more alert!

It's a Fact ✓

A bar of chocolate at break time gives you a quick sugar 'hit' and a brief spurt of energy for about half an hour. However, when this wears off the body's energy levels quickly drop, leaving you irritable and unable to concentrate. This is not helpful if you still have an hour until lunch. A snack such as a banana with less sugar and more complex carbohydrate will keep you going for longer.

Food and behaviour

Do you have food habits? Some people see food as a comfort. They eat when they feel stressed or when they are relaxing in front of the TV. Others turn to food when they are bored, or doing homework, or tired, or sitting on the bus home from school. But all this extra nibbling isn't healthy for most of us. And it doesn't help us deal with the stress or the boredom or the tiredness, either.

"I still want to be able to have a sweet treat sometimes."

"It's not the corn in popcorn that's bad for you — it's the oil and salt or sugary flavouring."

"My mum says a glass of milk is the perfect snack."

"I eat when I'm bored. It gives me something to do."

New habits?

Sometimes we think we are hungry when in fact we are thirsty. The next time you feel like a snack, have a drink of water instead and see if it makes a difference. Alternatively, phone a friend or go for a bike ride. A change of activity may be all that is needed to take away the urge to snack.

If you like to eat while watching TV or doing homework, how about munching on a handful of raisins or some carrot sticks rather than some of the less healthy products advertised during the commercial breaks?

A glass of water can take away the urge to snack. It is also calorie-free and it won't rot your teeth.

BODY IMAGE

People come in all shapes and sizes. Tall or short, wide-hipped or narrow-shouldered, flat-footed or knobbly-kneed. We inherit many of these physical characteristics from our parents. They are part of who we are.

Of course, someone can change their shape to a certain extent through diet or exercise. The proportion of fat and muscle in the body can be altered in this way, and pages 32-35 deal with obesity and dieting. But often body image has nothing to do with how healthy we are. It is to do with how we feel about our bodies.

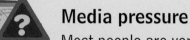

What Would you do?

Your best friend is unhappy because she thinks her thighs are too big. Do you:

a) commiserate with her, saying yours are too big too;

b) tell her that she is being ridiculous;

c) say something positive, e.g. she has fantastic skin/eyes/smile?

Turn to page 47 for the answers.

Media pressure

Most people are very good at saying what they don't like about their bodies. Images of tall, thin, beautiful people on TV and in magazines seem to suggest that we should all strive for such unrealistic body shapes. The pressure to look a certain way can feel overwhelming. However, it is important to remember that a model's body shape is not normal, or typical, and may have been achieved through excessive dieting that can cause serious health problems such as weak bones (osteoporosis) and reduced fertility.

How do you feel when you see images of skinny models and celebrities?

Changes at puberty

During puberty, a young person's body changes in all sorts of ways. Boys and girls have a growth 'spurt'. Girls' hips widen, and the layer of fat that women store beneath the skin typically increases at this time. Boys develop more muscle and their shoulders broaden.

But not everyone develops at the same rate, or in the same way. Puberty is a time when our body shape becomes more individual, more distinctive. Every person needs to value their body shape, as it is part of what makes them unique.

Help yourself

Tips to achieve a more positive body image:

- Write down three things you like about your body.
- Go for a brisk walk — you'll feel much better about yourself!
- Look for role models who have a body shape like yours.
- Make yourself a tasty fruit salad and let all those vitamins and minerals get to work building healthy, glowing skin, strong nails and shiny hair.

The pressure to conform to an 'ideal' body shape can be very strong. When you look in the mirror, remember to focus on what you like about yourself.

OBESITY

Obesity means being seriously overweight. Unlike shoe size or height, obesity is not something we necessarily inherit from our parents. There are a number of different reasons why people become obese, but all involve consuming more calories than the body burns. These extra calories are stored as fat.

Today the average British schoolchild is 8-10cm fatter around the waist than 20 years ago.

Obesity and health

Everyone stores some fat beneath their skin and around their internal organs, but too much fat causes several health problems. Obese people are at greater risk from heart disease, diabetes, arthritis, indigestion and some cancers. Obesity is most effectively reduced through a combination of diet (eating fewer calories) and exercise (burning more calories).

A growing problem

Obesity has become a serious and growing problem in the developed world. This is due to the fact that many of us eat more calories than we need. Food is more readily available now than in the past, and much of it is high in fat and sugar. Bigger portions, junk food and high-fat snacks all play a part. However, the problem is made worse by the increasing lack of physical activity in daily life.

Driving rather than walking, sitting rather than moving, using the internet rather than going out all mean that our bodies burn fewer calories.

WHAT'S THE PROBLEM?

'I think I'm obese. My friends tease me about my weight. I don't know what to do.'

If you think you might be seriously overweight, the best thing you can do is talk to your doctor about it. He or she will weigh you and measure your height, and from this work out your Body Mass Index (BMI) which indicates whether you have a problem or not. If you are found to be overweight, your doctor can then give you advice that is tailored to your age, needs and lifestyle.

Sometimes increasing the amount of physical activity you do can make all the difference as your body begins to burn off some of the extra calories it has been storing as fat. Sport is a good way to make new friends, too — friends who respect you for who you are.

All kinds of physical activity help to reduce excess fat. Join a club or exercise with your friends and you'll have fun, too.

It's a Fact

The number of overweight children in developed countries is rising fast. The International Obesity Taskforce estimates that one in five children in Europe is now overweight.

DIETING

How many times have you heard people say that they are 'going on a diet'? Dieting means controlling what we eat. But how effective is this as a way to lose excess weight? And is it good for us?

Burn the fat

An overweight or obese person stores a potentially dangerous amount of fat in the body. Reducing this amount of fat will bring all sorts of health benefits. Nutrition experts agree that the way to do this is to eat fewer calories and increase physical activity so that the body is forced to burn the energy that has been stored as fat.

The metabolic rate

However, eating fewer calories does not mean going hungry, or starving. If someone deprives themselves of essential nutrients, including carbohydrates, the body reacts by slowing down in order to conserve energy. It reduces the metabolic rate, which is the rate at which our bodies burn energy.

Help yourself

Cutting excess calories

Sometimes we don't have to adjust our eating habits very much in order to cut down on our intake of excess calories. If you eat quickly then your stomach doesn't have time to recognise that it has had enough. Eat slowly and you may find you don't want that second helping, after all!

If all you do is eat fewer fatty and sugary foods and replace them with more vegetables and wholegrain carbohydrates you will notice the difference.

The best way to lose weight is to eat fewer fatty, sugary foods and replace them with more nutrient-rich, high-fibre foods such as vegetables and whole grains. This type of diet, when combined with regular exercise, actually increases the metabolic rate, so more fat is burned. It is also healthier because the body is not being deprived of essential nutrients.

Bad diets

Fancy eating nothing but cabbage for a fortnight? How about the banana diet? Or what about cutting out all carbohydrates? There are all sorts of 'fad' diets and 'miracle' diets around, but most are designed to make money for their inventors and tend to involve measures that deprive the body of essential nutrients.

There is no 'quick fix' for losing weight. Studies show that dieters who aim to lose half a kilogram each week through a well-balanced low-fat diet and exercise plan are more likely to keep the weight off than someone who buys into the 'Lose 3kg in five days!' variety. A good diet isn't one that leaves you feeling miserable and hungry all the time. It means eating what you need to stay fit and healthy.

What Would you do?

You've been advised to lose a bit of weight. Do you:

a) go on a strict diet for a short period;
b) change your eating habits so that you eat more healthily and save sweet or fatty treats for special occasions;
c) vow never to eat anything sweet or fatty again?

Turn to page 47 for the answers.

HAVE YOUR SAY

"I like big portions, but now I have a big plate of pasta and vegetables instead of a big plate of chips."

"I lost weight when I started walking to school."

ANOREXIA

Anorexia nervosa is a serious eating disorder. People with anorexia have an intense fear of gaining weight. They usually have a distorted body image and try to control their eating through excessive dieting. Their mental and physical well-being is affected.

Causes

The causes of anorexia are complex and not fully understood, but anorexia most commonly takes hold as young people enter their teenage years. This is a time when young people become more aware of body shape, and may be unduly influenced by the pressure to look a certain way. However, plenty of people diet without becoming anorexic. Experts have identified certain triggers such as low self-esteem, family and exam pressures that may push an anxious teenager into obsessive and extreme behaviour.

Symptoms

Many people with anorexia try to mask their altered eating habits, so symptoms can be hard to detect. However, progressive weight loss coupled with tiredness, constipation or diarrhoea, fainting, brittle hair and rough skin, and a marked change in behaviour

around food (often obsessive) are all common symptoms. So too is excessive exercising and use of laxatives and/or vomiting to avoid the digestion of food.

Poor body image and low self-esteem contribute to anorexia.

HAVE YOUR SAY

"More girls than boys get anorexia, but my cousin Michael had it."

"It's my body. No one can tell me what to eat."

Long-term effects

Estimates suggest that anorexia leads to death in 10-15 per cent of sufferers. This is usually a result of starvation, dehydration, the weakening of muscles around the heart leading to a heart attack, or the prolonged absence of essential minerals. Other damage includes brittle bones (osteoporosis), reduced fertility in men and women, and low blood pressure. Nevertheless, people with anorexia can be helped by trained experts who try to understand its causes as well as treat its symptoms.

People with anorexia need expert help to overcome the impulse to starve themselves.

WHAT'S THE PROBLEM?

'My friend has recently stopped eating in front of me. She worries all the time about her weight, even though she's not fat, but she wears baggy clothes so it is difficult to tell if she has lost weight. She seems depressed and I'm worried that she might have anorexia.'

You obviously care about your friend and she may appreciate the opportunity to talk things over with you. However, if she is anorexic she needs professional help. Sometimes anorexics are very good at hiding their symptoms from adults. You may be the only one who has noticed these changes and telling her parents, or a teacher, or the school nurse or counsellor is almost certainly the best thing you can do for her. With the right help she is more likely to make a full recovery.

BULIMIA

Bulimia is an eating disorder. People with bulimia 'binge' or consume huge amounts of food – often junk foods high in sugar and fat. This is followed by a period of purging, which means getting rid of the food before it is digested by vomiting or using laxatives to expel it from the digestive tract.

Causes

As with anorexia, the causes of bulimia are complex and not fully understood. Poor self-image, low self-esteem and the pressure to look a certain way all play a part. Traumatic events are also seen as triggers. Once the binge eating has taken place, the sufferer often feels overwhelmed by guilt which leads to the purging behaviour. They may also exercise excessively in an effort to 'undo' the binge. As the cycle of bingeing and purging is repeated, the illness becomes more difficult to control and the mental and physical stress increases.

It's a Fact ✓

Statistics on bulimia and anorexia vary because many cases go unreported, but estimates suggest that about 3 per cent of girls and young women and 0.5 - 1 per cent of boys and young men suffer from some kind of eating disorder.

People with bulimia feel trapped in a cycle of binge eating, guilt, depression and purging.

Symptoms

Bulimia can be particularly difficult to detect because, unlike anorexia, many sufferers stay roughly the same weight. Binge eating is often done in private, away from other people, and so too is the purging. However, teeth problems are common as the acid from the vomiting can cause serious decay. Many bulimics also show signs of depression. Sufferers typically feel lonely, isolated and ashamed. However, it is important to remember that bulimia is a disease and if you think someone may be affected, the best thing you can do is encourage them to seek professional medical help. If it goes untreated, bulimia can cause irreversible damage to some internal organs.

Help yourself

Ask for help

Surveys suggest that many children and young people are reluctant to tell their parents if they have problems with food. However, feelings of guilt, low self-esteem and fear of not being taken seriously are all part of the problem. Getting support from adults (parents or a counsellor or health professionals) is really important if the sufferer is to make a good recovery.

People may binge eat foods they know to be less healthy, which only increases their feelings of guilt.

FOOD ALLERGIES AND INTOLERANCES

Most of us are able to eat a huge variety of foods without ever suffering from a nasty reaction. However, some people have to be very careful about what they eat. Perhaps you know someone with a peanut allergy, or coeliac disease? Food allergies and intolerances are becoming increasingly common, and symptoms can range from mild irritation to life-threatening anaphylactic shock (see panel on page 41).

It's a Fact ✓

Coeliac disease affects approximately one in every 200 people. It is a lifelong condition in which the body's immune system reacts to a substance called gluten (found in wheat, barley, rye and oats), causing inflammation of the gut lining. This makes it difficult to digest food, depriving the body of essential nutrients. The only treatment is to stop eating gluten.

Food allergies

A food allergy develops when the body's defence system (the immune system) reacts to a food that it mistakenly believes is harmful. Every time this particular food is eaten, the immune system triggers one or more allergic symptoms ranging from the mild (tingling mouth, a rash or itchy skin) to the more serious (swelling, vomiting, a racing heart) to the potentially fatal (breathing problems, shock, heart failure). Foods that may produce some of these reactions include nuts, wheat, egg white and shellfish.

Food intolerances

A food intolerance is a reaction to a particular food that does not involve the immune system. Symptoms can range from digestive discomfort to skin problems and tiredness but they are rarely life-threatening. Lactose intolerance, for example, is where the lactose found in cow's milk cannot be absorbed through the intestines, causing bowel irritation and diarrhoea. Other intolerances include adverse reactions to alcohol, caffeine and some food additives.

This patient is being tested for a range of food allergies. A tiny drop of each allergen is put on an area of skin on her arm. A rash will signal an allergic reaction.

Diagnosis and treatment

Anyone who thinks that they may have a food allergy or intolerance should ask their doctor's advice. Allergies can be diagnosed through specific medical tests. Food intolerances can be more difficult to diagnose, and your doctor will probably ask you to keep a food diary, listing what you eat and how you feel afterwards. The best way to treat food allergies and intolerances is to avoid the foods that cause them. Most packaging now indicates if it contains food that may cause an allergic reaction.

WHAT'S THE PROBLEM?

'What is anaphylactic shock and why does it happen?'

Anaphylactic shock is an extreme type of allergic reaction, most frequently caused by peanuts or non-food substances such as bee stings. The body rapidly produces a huge amount of dangerous chemicals that cause muscles to contract, blood pressure to drop and the throat to swell, cutting off air to the lungs. It requires an immediate injection of adrenalin to reverse these symptoms, and people who know they are at risk usually carry a ready-filled adrenalin injector such as an EpiPen.

FOOD HYGIENE

Salmonella, E.coli, Listeria... these are just some of the germs that can contaminate our food. Food hygiene is about avoiding these germs. A few basic rules can make all the difference between food that is good for us, and food that makes us sick.

Germs and bacteria

Some foods such as raw meats already have harmful bacteria in them. The only way to destroy this bacteria is to cook the food right through at a high temperature. Other foods pick up bacteria from the environment they are in. All bacteria spreads rapidly in a moist, warm atmosphere. Fresh or cooked food should be covered and stored in the fridge or the freezer to slow down the spread of bacteria. However, be aware that freezing food does not kill existing bacteria. Only cooking will do this.

What Would you do?

You are going on a picnic. What kind of sandwiches will you take?

a) homemade chicken sandwiches
b) shop-bought and sealed ham sandwiches
c) homemade salad sandwiches.

Turn to page 47 for the answers.

These girls are learning about hygiene in a food technology class.

Have a look inside your fridge at home. Are all the contents stored as hygienically as possible?

Help yourself

Dos and don'ts

Here are a few basic things to remember about food hygiene. You may be able to think of others.

- Wash your hands before touching food.
- Wash all fruits and vegetables under running water before eating or cooking them.
- Always follow the cooking and storage instructions on food packets and labels.
- Do not eat meat and dairy products that have passed their use-by date.
- Never leave cooked food standing at room temperature for more than two hours.
- Cover and refrigerate or freeze cooked food if you don't want to eat it straight away.
- Keep raw meat and fish away from cooked food to prevent contamination.
- Wash used utensils and surfaces with hot soapy water or with an anti-bacterial cleaner such as diluted bleach.

Keep it clean

Not all bacteria comes from food. Harmful bacteria can be passed to food from dirty hands, or dirty kitchen utensils, towels and worktops. Always wash your hands before preparing food, and thoroughly clean utensils and work surfaces that have been used to prepare meat in hot soapy water in order to kill off any lingering germs.

Keep it separate

Cover all food that you store in the fridge. This will prevent bacteria spreading from one food to another. Don't pile different foods on top of each other, and be particularly careful to store uncooked meat at the bottom of the fridge so that it doesn't contaminate other foods.

MAKE IT, EAT IT!

Now you have learned about healthy eating, a balanced diet and food hygiene, it's time to get cooking. Preparing your own food not only ensures that additives and saturated fats are kept to a minimum, it also makes eating more fun!

Remember the healthy eating plate on page 12? The following recipes all use foods from different food groups, with an emphasis on variety and taste. You might like to start a recipe book of your own, creating new dishes with your favourite ingredients as part of a nutritious, well-balanced diet.

Vegetable kebabs

Wash some tomatoes, green pepper chunks and baby sweet corn and thread them onto some stainless steel skewers. Brush with a little olive oil, add pepper to taste and toast under a moderate grill for about 10 minutes, turning frequently. These kebabs are full of fibre and vitamins and they're colourful too.

Baked chilli chicken

Peel and finely chop a clove of garlic and stir into 100ml plain low fat yoghurt along with half a teaspoon of chilli powder, 1 teaspoon of paprika and 1 teaspoon of tomato puree. Place 2 x 150g pieces of skinless chicken breast into a baking dish, smear over the yoghurt mixture and bake in a pre-heated oven at 180º/gas mark 4 for about 40 minutes. Serve with rice for a tasty dish of low-fat protein and complex carbohydrate.

For a vegetarian alternative, replace the chicken with slices of extra-firm tofu (a soya bean product packed with protein).

HAVE YOUR SAY

"On Sundays I make pancakes with chopped bananas."

"I didn't think I liked avocados until I made my own guacamole."

"I've cooked a whole meal for my family!"

"For a quick pasta sauce, fry some chopped onion and garlic and add a carton of sieved tomatoes."

Apricot flapjacks

The oats and apricots are full of complex carbohydrate and fibre but these flapjacks are high in sugar and fat too so keep as an occasional treat.

Place 75g of reduced-fat butter or margarine, 50g of dark brown sugar and 2 tablespoons of golden syrup into a shallow microwavable dish and cook on high for 2 minutes. Remove and mix in 150g of porridge oats and 40g of chopped dried apricots. Press the mixture down with the back of a fork and then cook in the microwave for a further 3 minutes. Mark into squares and leave to cool.

These flapjacks are made with apricots, but you could use a handful of nuts or raisins instead.

Fruit cocktail

You can make a fruit cocktail out of any fruits, but try choosing four or five of your favourites, with a variety of colours and textures for maximum vitamins, minerals and fibre. A base of apple or pear chunks and some orange or satsuma pieces works well, while slices of kiwi or a handful of blueberries add contrast. Strawberries, slices of banana or fresh pineapple provide sweetness and peaches are great too. Alternatively, you could whizz them all up into a custom-made fruit smoothie.

Create your own fruit cocktail recipe. The possibilities are endless!

Glossary

absorption the process by which food molecules pass from the intestines into the bloodstream

additives substances added to food to make it last longer or taste stronger or look better

anorexia a disorder where sufferers deprive themselves of food

binge eating eating excessive amounts of food in a short time

bulimia a disorder where sufferers binge-eat then try to get rid of the calories by vomiting or using laxatives or by exercising excessively

calorie a unit of energy

cholesterol a substance found in fat; bad for the heart

diabetes a condition that occurs when the body stops being able to process sugar properly

diet what we eat

digestion the process by which the food we eat is broken down inside the body

enzymes acids in the body required for digestion

fair trade food food for which farmers have been paid a fair price

fibre aids a healthy gut; found in all fruit, vegetables, seeds and wholegrains

food allergy when the body reacts to a food it mistakenly believes is harmful

food intolerance a mild adverse reaction to a particular food

GM genetically modified

halal a method of meat production used by Muslims

hydrogenated fat oil that has been processed

indigestion discomfort after eating too much or too quickly

junk food unhealthy food

kosher a Jewish custom where dairy and meat products are prepared and eaten separately

metabolic rate the rate at which the body burns energy

minerals a group of nutrients; each type of mineral does a different job in the body

molecule tiny particle

monosodium glutamate a salty additive

nutrients food molecules; proteins, carbohydrates, fats, minerals and vitamins

obese seriously overweight

organic produced without artificial pesticides or fertilizers

processed food food that has been pre-prepared outside the home

protein needed for growth and repair in the body

pulses peas, beans and lentils

Ramadan the Muslim month of fasting and prayer

salmonella a dangerous bacteria found in uncooked chicken

saturated fats fats that are found in meat and dairy produce

tofu protein-rich food made from soya beans

vegan someone who doesn't eat any animal products, including eggs and dairy

vitamins a group of nutrients; each type of vitamin does a different job in the body

whole grain cereals, rice and flour containing every bit of the grain

Further information

USEFUL ORGANIZATIONS AND WEBSITES

www.eatwell.gov.uk/info/games/

The site of the Food Standards Agency with lots of interactive games for kids, including 'Germ Travel' and 'Unmuddle the Meals'.

www.lifebytes.gov.uk/eating/eat_menu.html

Plenty of tips and stories about weight watching, healthy eating, hygiene and a quiz for Keystage 3 children.

www.vegsoc.org/

The website for The Vegetarian Society, with information, recipes, and news about vegetarian issues.

www.news.bbc.co.uk/cbbcnews/hi/guides

Click on 'eating problems', 'obesity' or 'food allergies' for lots of helpful tips, advice and information.

www.kidsandcooking.co.uk/ KidsRecipesCategory.html

Lots of fun, child-friendly recipes, including an egg-free cake for children with allergies and recipes for meat and vegetarian alternatives.

What would you do?

Page 5: Chocolate is full of sugar and fat, and too much of this type of food is bad for you. Eating it will make you less hungry for your dinner, which probably contains the healthier types of food your body needs. But maybe you skipped lunch and now you're starving. Maybe it is a 'new' type of bar and you want to try it. Or maybe you are worried about gaining weight. Different factors will influence your decision.

Page 12: Everyone needs breakfast. If you don't eat you'll soon feel hungry. However, a snack bar from a vending machine isn't a healthy choice because it probably contains too much sugar, giving you a quick energy 'hit' followed by a big loss of energy after an hour or so. Fried bacon and eggs will fill you up and provide you with plenty of protein, but they also contain a lot of fat. A bowl of cereal, a drink of water and some fruit is the best option, as the complex carbohydrates in the cereal should keep you going all morning, and the water, milk and fruit will stop you dehydrating and provide essential vitamins and minerals.

Page 19: Choosing option (c) will almost certainly take your fat and salt consumption over the recommended daily amount. However, a processed 'low-fat' variety will still contain additives and not enough fibre or vitamins. A homemade pizza may take a little longer to prepare, but you can customize it yourself and it will be much better for you. Try a taste test, comparing it to the frozen variety. What differences do you notice? What about cost?

Page 22: (a) means that you'll be hungry, and you won't have done anything to help yourself the next time you are offered fish. Choose (c) and you won't feel hungry, but is smothering food in ketchup such a great idea? Ask yourself why you 'hate' fish. It is a healthy source of protein and many essential vitamins and minerals. Is it that particular recipe you don't like? What if it was cooked in a different way? Choose (b) to play the taste game...

Page 27: All three meals contain complex carbohydrates, fibre, fat and protein but (b) contains more essential vitamins and minerals.

Page 30: It may be that your friend's perception of her thighs is inaccurate, if she is comparing herself to pictures of unrealistically skinny celebrities. However, even if her thighs are larger than the average person's, she needs to feel more positive about herself. What are her 'best' features? Make sure you remind her of them!

Page 35: With (a) you will probably lose some weight, but what happens when the diet stops? The likelihood is that you will simply put the weight back on. However, (c) may be an unrealistic goal for you – don't set yourself up to fail! (b) is likely to be the most effective, healthy and happy option for you over time.

Page 42: Is it a hot day? Can you keep the sandwiches cool? Sealed or unsealed, temperature is crucial. Chicken or ham sandwiches should be okay if they aren't going to sit in a warm bag or lunchbox for more than two hours. If you're not sure, make salad sandwiches but take care to wash the salad first.

INDEX

Numbers in bold refer to illustrations.